A M E R I C A N   T R A I L S

EASTERN TRAILS
From Footpaths to Turnpikes

EASTERN TRAILS
From Footpaths to Turnpikes

KATHY PELTA

Published by Raintree Steck-Vaughn Publishers, an imprint of Steck-Vaughn Company

Raintree Steck-Vaughn Publishers Staff

Publishing Director: Walter Kossmann   Project Manager: Lyda Guz
Editor: Shirley Shalit   Electronic Production: Scott Melcer
Photo Editor: Margie Foster

Library of Congress Cataloging-in-Publication Data
Pelta, Kathy.
    Eastern trails from footpaths to turnpikes / by Kathy Pelta.
        p.   cm.– (American trails)
    Summary: Traces the building of roads in the eastern part of the United States from the time of the earliest colonists to the 1850s.
    ISBN 0-8172-4071-3
    1. East (U.S.) – Historical geography – Juvenile literature.   2. Trails – East (U.S.) – History – Juvenile literature.   3. Roads – East (U.S.) – History – Juvenile literature. [1. Roads – United States – History.]   I. Title.   II. Series.
    E179.5.P36   1997
    974 – dc21   96-46809
                                                                                    CIP   AC

Printed and bound in the United States

1 2 3 4 5 6 7 8 9 0 LB 01 00 99 98 97

Acknowledgments

The author and publisher would like to thank the following for photos and illustrations. Cover (inset) Corbis-Bettmann, (map) Westlight; p. 3 Culver Pictures; pp. 6, 7 © Superstock; p. 9 courtesy New York Power Authority; p. 10 Brown Brothers; pp. 12, 13 The Granger Collection; pp. 15, 16, 20 North Wind Picture Archives; p. 21 Brown Brothers; p. 24 The Granger Collection; p. 27 Culver Pictures; p. 30 North Wind Picture Archives; p. 32 Corbis-Bettmann; p. 34 Brown Brothers; p. 35 North Wind Picture Archives; p. 39 Culver Pictures; p. 42 State Historical Society of Wisconsin; pp. 43, 44, 45, 47 The Granger Collection; p. 48 UPI/Corbis-Bettmann; p. 53 North Wind Picture Archives; p. 55 Culver Pictures; p. 59 North Wind Picture Archives; p. 60 Washington University Gallery of Art, St. Louis, Gift of Nathaniel Phillips, Boston, 1890; p. 64 UPI/Corbis-Bettmann; p. 65 Corbis-Bettmann; p. 67 Culver Pictures; p. 69 North Wind Picture Archives; p. 70 © Runk/Schoenberger/Grant Heilman Photography; p. 75 New Orleans Museum of Art, Gift of Mr. William E. Groves; p. 76 © Andre Jenny/Unicorn Stock Photos; p. 77 The Granger Collection; pp. 79, 81 North Wind Picture Archives; p. 83 Woolaroc Museum.

Cartography: GeoSystems, Inc.

Contents

North American Trails

Long before any Europeans arrived in North America there were trails winding through the woods and wilderness, and across the dry stretches of desert. Some paths were shortcuts that animals took to salt licks. Others led to favorite water holes. Native Americans used such paths— or created their own—as they hunted and gathered food, made pilgrimages to sacred sites, and traded with neighbors or fought with enemies.

The first Europeans to explore the interior of North America traveled along rivers and bays by boat, or followed existing trails over land. Often, with the help of native guides, the explorers also blazed new trails. In time, favorite land trails were widened to accommodate oxcarts

Much of the eastern United States in the 1600s was forest-covered like this landscape in the Blue Ridge Mountains of North Carolina today.

and horse-drawn wagons. Soon stagecoaches and over-land express wagons were rumbling over the improved roads, and eventually came motorcars. Some trails became routes for railroad lines.

The nation's trails reflected its history. The earliest European pathfinders were the Spanish. In the 1500s they claimed much of what is now the United States. By the 1800s, Spanish trails linked Catholic missions, military posts, and pueblos (towns) in the southeast, the southwest, and along the California coast.

In the 1600s, a century after the Spanish first came to North America, people from other parts of Europe settled along the Atlantic coast north of Spanish Florida. As they moved inland, they, too, used existing trails or

This western Virginia scene must look much like it did when the English first started settling the area.

blazed their own. In the late 1700s, when the English colonies became the United States of America, the people of the new nation had created a network of roads and paths that covered the eastern one-third of the continent, extending as far west as the Mississippi River. This is the story of the early eastern trails and those people who used them.

Moving Inland

The first Europeans to arrive in what is now the eastern United States and Canada often found land travel difficult, especially in the north with its dense woods, harsh winters, and muddy spring season. The newcomers often chose to travel over "water trails," rather than follow one of the many Indian land trails that crisscrossed the region.

Those who settled near the coast or along rivers used boats or canoes to go places. So did the traders and trappers who ventured farther inland. French explorers Louis Joliet, a fur trader, and Jacques Marquette, a Catholic priest and missionary, traveled south in their birch canoes all the way from Lake Michigan to the mouth of the Arkansas River on the Mississippi River!

Settlers had already claimed most of the land near water by the time the second wave of Europeans arrived in the northeast. These newcomers had to find places to live farther inland and away from rivers. For them, boats were not the handiest way to travel. Instead, they used land trails of the Eastern Woodlands Indians. They followed the trails of the Shawnee, the Iroquois, the Algonquin, the Narragansett, the Delaware, the Miami, the Erie, and many more. These inland settlers also blazed their own trails clearing the dense woods to make pathways between their

This Thomas Hart Benton mural depicts the Iroquois people greeting European immigrants as they arrive on the shore of the St. Lawrence River.

wilderness communities. Over the years, these paths were widened and straightened to become roads used by later emigrants as well as soldiers, mail carriers, farmers, and peddlers. By 1840, the network of roads and trails that started in the east had pushed the frontier of the new United States west to the Mississippi River.

ONE

Early Trails
in the East

Virginia

Late in April of 1607, after a four-month journey from England, 120 colonists in three small ships sailed into Chesapeake Bay in what is now the state of Virginia. They had been sent by the London Company, investors who expected the transplanted English to make a profit for the company—from trade, or by finding gold, or by discovering a passage to the East Indies. Near the mouth of the James River the colonists came ashore, and within a

Jamestown might have looked like this in 1622. This drawing appeared in a pamphlet published in Holland in 1707.

JAMESTOWN IN 1622
VIRGINIA

A Short Stay in Maine

In 1607, the same year the Jamestown colony was started in Virginia, Captain George Popham brought a shipload of English colonists to the mouth of the Sagadahoc River (now the Kennebec River) on the coast of present-day Maine. As was the case in the Virginia colony, the mission for the Popham colonists was to find a passage to the East Indies, and to establish trade with the Native Americans. Although the trade in furs was brisk enough, the colonists discovered they could only take a boat as far inland as the falls on the Sagadahoc (near what is now Augusta, Maine), which dashed any hope of finding a water route across North America to the East Indies. So after one bitterly cold winter the Popham colonists built another ship—the first oceangoing vessel ever built by English people in America—and returned to England.

month had built a fort on a low, swampy island. This became Jamestown, the first permanent English colony in the New World. Although a Shawnee trail led west into the mountains most early Virginia settlers remained in the coastal lowlands.

The Jamestown colony barely managed to survive the miserably cold and wet climate, Indian attacks, near-starvation, and many deaths from malaria, dysentery, and other diseases. For food, the people depended on trading with the Native Americans for corn. On one such trading trip, Captain John Smith, the colony's leader, nearly lost his life. After sailing up the Chickahominy River, he was captured by Chief Powhatan's braves. At the last minute he was saved from execution by the pleading of Powhatan's daughter, Pocahontas.

Since the local Native Americans had little to trade except corn, the Jamestown colonists had to give up their plan to run a trading post. Instead, they looked for products to ship to England, to justify the expense of their voyage. Finding no gold (and no passage to the East Indies), they turned to the forests for products to satisfy the London Company. From cedar wood they made clapboards (large planks used for siding on wooden houses) and from pine they made turpentine and tar.

Then they started to raise the tobacco plant, whose leaves proved to be the most profitable product of all.

The Virginians sold their tobacco to buyers in England who turned it into pipe tobacco or snuff—pulverized tobacco that could be inhaled. Soon, many tobacco plantations were established, generally on Chesapeake Bay or on one of the rivers that flowed into the bay. As a result, the Virginia colonists could do much of their traveling over waterways. Although a Shawnee trail led west into the mountains, most early Virginia settlers remained in the coastal lowlands. Since nearly every plantation near the coast had a boat landing, the farmers did not need to haul their tobacco long distances over a road to a market town. They simply rolled the large barrels of tobacco down to their own wharves and loaded them onto sailing ships bound for England. For the plantation owners, these "rolling roads" between plantations and waterways were the only roads they needed. If a plantation was located farther inland, the owner cut a rolling road through the forest to the nearest river or bay where the tobacco could

A Virginia wharf of the eighteenth century with barrels of tobacco ready for shipment is shown in this colored engraving.

be loaded onto a ship. Then, after curing (drying) the tobacco he packed it into huge casks, or barrels with spikes driven through them that served as axles. The gang of hardy workers who pushed and tumbled the casks along the bumpy rolling road were called tobacco rollers. Since a 50-mile trip could take as long as two weeks, the tobacco rollers nailed a box of provisions to the shafts that were the barrels' axles. Each night they would make camp, frying their bacon and cooking their hoecakes (like pancakes) over an open fire, and then sleeping under the stars.

To protect against Indian attacks, in 1645 the Virginia settlers built a military fort and trading post at the edge of the Blue Ridge Mountains. Named Fort Henry, this post marked Virginia's western frontier for many years. Before 1700 only a handful of adventurous hunters and fur traders left the coast to explore what they called the "Old West"–the lands beyond the flat Virginia plain known as the Tidewater. Starting from Fort Henry, these explorers set off on a Shawnee trail that led over the Blue Ridge Mountains and into the valley of the Shenandoah River. But years passed before very many of the Virginia settlers followed the Shawnee trail west.

New York

Shortly after Captain John Smith mapped parts of the American coast and Chesapeake Bay, another Englishman, Henry Hudson, somehow got his hands on those maps. In 1609, two years after the founding of Jamestown, Hudson set sail from The Netherlands (Holland), in the Dutch ship *Half Moon* with a crew of Dutch and English sailors. He had a contract with the Dutch East India Company to find a way to the East Indies from the eastern coast of North America. The Dutch East India Company was formed to encourage Dutch trade in the Far East.

Henry Hudson arrived in what is now the state of New York in the fall of 1609 and made his way slowly up the river that later carried his name. The journey to what is now Albany, New York, took eight days. Hudson used the tide flowing upriver twice each day to push his boat. When the tide turned and flowed south toward the sea, he anchored against the strong current. While waiting in the low water for the next tidal surge, Hudson and his crew made friends with the Mohawk and other Iroquois who lived along the river, trading beads, knives, and hatchets for their tobacco, corn, and beaver and otter skins.

Since *Half Moon* was flying the Dutch flag, the Dutch claimed this great river valley as theirs. They called it New Netherland. Within a few years they had started a colony, and before long Dutch traders were bringing manufactured goods upriver by boat to trade with the Native Americans. The Dutch put up a trading post, Fort Orange, near present-day

The French in Canada and the Midwest

In 1608, a year before Henry Hudson made his slow way up the Hudson River in *Half Moon*, the French explorer Samuel de Champlain set up a trading post at what became the town of Quebec. It was the first permanent French settlement in North America. Soon after, Champlain founded Montreal. These two outposts on the St. Lawrence River were the start of the colony of New France—now Canada. Half a century later, the French explorer La Salle visited parts of the Ohio Valley. A few years after that, French explorers Louis Joliet and Father Jacques Marquette paddled their canoes down the Mississippi to the mouth of the Arkansas River to secure France's claim to the entire Mississippi River valley. For the next 75 years, until 1763, the French were a constant threat to the English colonies. Then the French and Indian War erupted. In that war the English defeated the French and claimed these lands for themselves.

Father Marquette is shown in this print signaling a Native American group with a peace pipe.

New Amsterdam looked like this in the mid-1600s while
it was still under the control of the Dutch.

Albany where they offered their brightly-colored beads,
cotton cloth, knives, and rum for the Native Americans'
valuable beaver and mink pelts.

Dutch colonists who settled near Fort Orange in 1624
found no easy way to reach the area over land. So they, too,
came by boat. A year later the Dutch established a trading
post 150 miles to the south at the mouth of the Hudson
River. They called it New Amsterdam (now New York).
Immediately the Hudson River became the "water trail" the
Dutch used to travel from one outpost to the other.

The tiny fur post of New Amsterdam grew faster than
Fort Orange. In a few years it had become a bustling town
of 300 residents—shopkeepers, blacksmiths, carpenters,
shoemakers, and sailmakers. At the edge of town lived
farmers. Ships crowded New Amsterdam's harbor, a con-
venient halfway point for vessels sailing the coastal waters
between the English colony in Virginia and the English

colonies set up in what is now Massachusetts after 1620.

Ships also plied the "water trail" up and down the Hudson between New Amsterdam and Fort Orange. Although there was a narrow land trail beside the river, the most popular way to travel between the two Dutch settlements was still by boat.

When the early Dutch settlers did follow a trail, it was likely to be an Indian portage—an overland path between waterways. One such portage was the sandy path between Fort Orange and the Mohawk River. Settlers from Fort Orange followed this trail when they bought land on the Mohawk River from the Iroquois to start a new village. It later became the city of Schenectady.

In 1664 the English gained control of New Netherland. In honor of their duke of York and Albany, they renamed the colony New York. The English also changed New Amsterdam's name to New York, and Fort Orange became Albany. Both towns continued to grow. Albany now served as the colony's inland port.

Up to Albany

Despite occasional shallow places and the flow of the tides—which sent water surging upriver twice each day and then flowing back toward the sea—oceangoing vessels could sail all the way up the Hudson to Albany's docks to unload cargo from London or Paris. For the trip back downriver, they took on local goods —furs, lumber, flour, and potatoes, as well as cider, flax, and ginseng (a medicinal herb much valued in China). Many ships also hauled passengers, who sometimes brought along their livestock, tying cows, sheep, or other animals to the mast.

Soon other towns began to dot the shores of the Hudson River around New York and Albany, and along the Mohawk River west of Schenectady. Each river town had

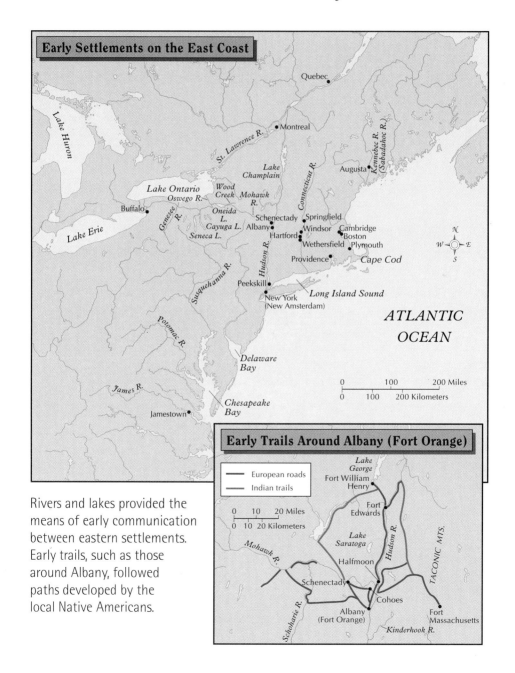

Early Settlements on the East Coast

Quebec

Lake Huron

St. Lawrence R.   Montreal

Lake Champlain

Kennebec R. (Sabadahoc R.)

Lake Ontario   Wood Creek   Augusta
Oswego R.   Mohawk R.

Connecticut R.

Buffalo   Oneida L.   Schenectady   Springfield
Genesee R.   Cayuga L.   Albany   Windsor   Cambridge
Lake Erie   Seneca L.   Hartford   Boston
Wethersfield   Plymouth

Hudson R.   Providence   Cape Cod

Susquehanna R.   Peekskill

New York
(New Amsterdam)   Long Island Sound

ATLANTIC
OCEAN

Potomac R.

Delaware Bay

| 0 | 100 | 200 Miles |
| 0 | 100 | 200 Kilometers |

James R.

Chesapeake Bay

Jamestown

Early Trails Around Albany (Fort Orange)

—— European roads
—— Indian trails

Lake George
Fort William Henry

Fort Edwards

| 0 | 10 | 20 Miles |
| 0 | 10 20 Kilometers |

Mohawk R.

Lake Saratoga

Hudson R.

TACONIC MTS.

Halfmoon

Schenectady

Cohoes

Schoharie R.

Albany
(Fort Orange)

Fort Massachusetts

Kinderhook R.

Rivers and lakes provided the means of early communication between eastern settlements. Early trails, such as those around Albany, followed paths developed by the local Native Americans.

its own well-used boat landing, since it was still easier to follow the "water trail" between settlements than to travel by land. Travelers went by canoe, or by *bateau*, a flat-bottomed boat barge that eight or ten men towed, or propelled through the water by rowing or pushing long poles against the shallow river bottom.

The need for overland trails came when New Yorkers began to settle far from waterways. When this happened, people followed Indian trails, which were generally the shortest and best routes. The old Iroquois Trail became the Great State Road connecting Albany in the east and Buffalo in the west. The road heading southwest from Albany to the Susquehanna River followed the Susquehanna Trail. The route from the town of Catskill on the Hudson to the Mohawk River followed what was once the old Catskill Trail. And in western New York, the north-south road along the Genesee River had once been the Genesee Trail of the Iroquois.

Following Indian trails made sense, for the native peoples knew well every part of their land. Their trails ran along thinly-wooded slopes that followed the natural curve of rivers. The trails were usually higher up, where the ground was drier. Here there was no underbrush but enough trees to shield travelers. Staying out of sight of possible enemies was as important to the colonists as to the tribes of the Iroquois Confederacy.

New England

Only a few years after the Dutch founded New Netherland and English colonists started Jamestown, English colonists also settled along the coast of what is now Massachusetts. The *Mayflower* Pilgrims started the town and colony of New Plymouth in 1620. Eight years later other Puritans

The Iroquois Trail

Before Europeans came to what is now New York, the Iroquois Trail led through the lands of the Five Nations Confederacy. The confederacy had once been five separate tribes, but with the help of the wise Hiawatha they became a single "family" around 1570. The Mohawk, the Onondaga, and the Seneca were considered the "elder brothers" of the

This totem or tribe-mark was developed for the Five Nations Confederacy.

Iroquois family. The Oneida and the Cayuga were the "younger brothers."

The people of the Five Nations Confederacy compared their lands to a "longhouse" where they all lived in peace and harmony. Their house was so big that it took many days to walk from one end to the other, and the Iroquois Trail made it easier for members to come together and make important decisions.

The trail started where the Mohawk and Hudson Rivers met, in the land of the Mohawks, keepers of the eastern door of the longhouse. The trail ran through the land of the Oneida to the land of Onondaga. They kept the permanent council fire—the great meeting place where leaders from each of the five nations would decide for peace, or for war with outsiders. The trail continued to the land of the Cayuga (near present Auburn, New York) and to the land of the Senecas, keepers of the western door of the longhouse.

from England formed Massachusetts Bay Colony with settlements around Boston. Like the Virginians, the Massachusetts colonists stayed near the coast, at first. They fished or traded or farmed, but rarely traveled inland and they felt no need for overland trails. If a pastor wanted to relocate his congregation, he chose a place close to Boston or one of the other coastal towns.

After a few years, however, Captain William Holmes and a few friends decided to leave Plymouth. They had heard the Wapanoag and other Algonquins describe a fertile land to the west, in the valley of the Connecticut River. Holmes and his friends wanted to go there and become traders. Rather than trying to travel overland through dense woods they went by boat, taking along wood framing for a house. On their water journey they circled around the tip of Cape Cod, passed into Long Island Sound, sailed along what is now the Connecticut coast, and then started up the Connecticut River. Forty miles upriver Holmes dropped anchor. The men brought the framework ashore, added

The settlement at Plymouth probably looked much like this for the first few years following the arrival of the first settlers on the *Mayflower*.

roof and siding, and Holmes had his trading post. Soon after, more Plymouth colonists came by sea to settle in this same part of the Connecticut valley.

Meanwhile around Boston other colonists began to talk of going west. They resented the strict Puritan rules of the Massachusetts Bay Colony and its governor, who gave the people little say on how their colony should be run. Finally in the spring of 1636 the Reverend Thomas Hooker and some other church leaders felt they could no longer endure living in the Boston area. They asked for permission to leave—moved, they said, by "a strong bent of their spirits for change."

Unlike the earlier emigrants from Plymouth, Thomas Hooker took his congregation west over land. From Cambridge he struck out through the wilderness. The people carried dishes, clothing, and other belongings on their backs. Through the woods they drove their pigs and goats and 160 head of cattle. Hooker's wife, too sick to walk, had to be carried on a stretcher.

Blue Laws

Sometimes colonists who fled the strict control of the religious leaders in Massachusetts Bay Colony became just as strict in their new colonies. In the 1600s many villages in New Haven Colony passed so-called "blue laws" about how people should behave. The village of Milford had a law that forbade a man from kissing his wife on the Sabbath. One Sunday a man broke the law. To escape punishment—a public lashing—he swam across the very wide Housatonic River to the town of Stratford. There, soon joined by his wife and family, he remained for the rest of his days, a leading citizen of the town.

Some of the time the emigrants pushed through tangled briar and dense forests, unsure where to go. But most of the way they tried to follow the Old Connecticut Path, the ancient east-west Indian trail that ran from Boston to Albany by way of what is now Springfield, Massachusetts.

Fourteen days after leaving their homes Hooker and his flock completed their 100-mile trek. They settled near Captain Holmes's trading post to found what is now the city of Hartford, Connecticut. Within the year, others from Massachusetts Bay arrived by the overland trail to establish the nearby communities of Wethersfield and Windsor. The people in these settlements joined with new settlers on the coast to form a colony called Connecticut—later, the state of Connecticut.

End of the Pocumtucks

In 1663 the Pocumtucks left their home on the Connecticut River in western Massachusetts to fight the Mohawks. To reach the Mohawks, they blazed a footpath west across the Appalachian Mountains from what is now Deerfield, Massachusetts, to present-day Troy, New York, on the Hudson River.

Dutch settlers in Fort Orange, across the Hudson from Troy, tried to end the war between the Mohawks and the Pocumtucks by working out a peace treaty. But as the Mohawk prince Saheda came over the trail to ratify the treaty he was murdered. This so angered the Mohawks that in a single day they killed every Pocumtuck warrior. From then on, the Pocumtucks lived in name only. Later, colonists from Massachusetts Bay Colony used this trail as they came west to settle in the valleys of the Hudson and Mohawk Rivers.

Roger Williams was sheltered by the Narragansett Indians during the
first winter after he left the Puritan colony in Massachusetts.

Shortly after Hooker's departure, another church leader,
Roger Williams, got into trouble with the Puritan authorities. Williams believed that church and state should be
separate. He also felt that people's religion was their business, not the government's. Furthermore, Roger Williams
dared to say that the Native Americans were the real owners of the land.

Such radical ideas infuriated the leaders of the colony.
But before they could bundle Williams onto a ship and
send him back to England, he fled into the woods. Roger

Williams worked his way south through freezing cold weather, following Indian trails when he could. He spent much of the winter living in the wigwams of his friends the Narragansett—whose language he spoke. In the early spring, Williams settled at the edge of Narragansett Bay. More exiles from Massachusetts Bay Colony followed Williams's path to join him and together they founded what came to be the town of Providence and the colony of Rhode Island.

In time, other colonists besides those out of favor with the authorities began to travel west and south. They followed the routes that Thomas Hooker, Roger Williams, and other early emigrants had taken. With more traffic in and around Boston, better paths were needed. Lawmakers ruled that each town near Boston must provide two or three of its citizens to help widen and straighten the footpaths to accommodate riders on horseback and horse-drawn wagons.

Portage to Lake Ontario

Long before the English settled what is now Rome, New York, the Iroquois had a portage trail there. They followed the trail as they carried their boats between the Mohawk River and Wood Creek, the waterway that led to Lake Ontario. The Iroquois called this portage De-o-wain-sta ("lifting or setting down the boat"). The mile-long trail was an important link in the water route between the Great Lakes region and the Atlantic Ocean.

When the French began to build forts in Canada in the early 1700s, the English worried about a French invasion from the north. So the English started building forts of their own—all on waterways reached by portage paths.

The road crews were reminded not to pull down anyone's house, or cut through a garden or orchard, or go where soil was wet and boggy.

After some years, many old Native American paths in New England had become main roads for the colonies. By the mid-1600s the Common Road opened between Boston and Providence, Rhode Island. South of Providence the name changed to Shore Road as it hugged the coastlines of Rhode Island and Connecticut on its way to the town of New York. By then, the Old Connecticut Path from Boston to Albany by way of Springfield was a well-used official road. From western Connecticut people followed another old Indian trail to Peekskill, New York, a town down the Hudson from Albany.

TWO

"The Mail Must Go Through": Early Post Roads

"Neither snow, nor rain, nor heat, nor gloom of night stays these couriers from the swift completion of their appointed rounds."

Inscription chiseled in stone on the front of the New York City Post Office

T he date was set: on January 1, 1673, a rider would leave New York on horseback to deliver mail to Boston over the new post road. The first official mail service in the English Colonies was about to begin!

A system of post roads for mail delivery in the colonies was the brainstorm of England's King Charles II. The year before, the king had asked New York's Governor Lovelace to plan a postal service with post roads. Until then, a merchant or government official who wanted to send important

An early postrider on the road between Worcester and Hartford.

papers or letters to a distant town hired a messenger to deliver them by horseback, racing along one of the narrow paths that were once Indian trails. Ordinary people who wanted to get word to someone far away had to send their message with a peddler or other traveler who happened to be going in that direction. Such good luck was rare.

Charges at Inns

An early postal regulation stated that no innkeeper was allowed to charge the postrider more than 2 shillings a bushel for oats and 4 pence for hay—whether he arrived by day or late at night.

To design a postal service, Governor Lovelace met with Connecticut's Governor Winthrop. The two agreed the postrider must be strong, healthy, and loyal. They would let him choose where people should deposit letters to be delivered by post.

The new post road was to follow existing trails between New York and Boston. The next step for the two governors was to hire workers to widen these trails to make them easier for the postrider to follow. The route from New York would hug the Connecticut coastline as far as New Haven, then turn north to Hartford and Springfield, Massachusetts. From there the post road would follow the well-traveled Old Connecticut Path to Boston.

Part of the roadmakers' job was to locate the best river crossings—either those with ferryboat operators, or those with water shallow enough for the rider to ford the stream. Also, there had to be taverns or inns along the trails where the postrider could rest and feed his horse or change horses.

Although the first postrider was scheduled to leave New York on January 1, things went awry. Dispatches from Albany that were to accompany the rest of the mail had not arrived. At last, after three weeks, they came. Quickly the governor's secretary stuffed the dispatches into the rider's saddlebag and sealed the bag with an official seal. Then the postrider galloped onto the post road. Two weeks later he arrived safely in Boston to deliver his mail and receive congratulations on the success of his journey.

From then on, a postrider left New York for Boston on the first Monday of each month—and was back in New York within the month. Although the axmen had done a good job of hacking away at the underbrush and fallen trees between settlements, the postrider sometimes had to do some clearing of his own. He carried the mail for New York, Hartford, and Boston in separate sealed saddlebags to be left at these main drop-off points. In an open bag he carried letters and packets addressed to places in-between. For his work, the postrider earned an annual salary plus a percentage of the charge for delivering letters and small packages. In the early years of the postal service, letters were sent "collect"—with the receiver paying the postage. This ensured that the mail was actually delivered. The amount of postage depended on the number of pages in the letter and how far it was going.

Colonists were pleased with their new mail system. For the first time, they could count on regular long-distance mail delivery. The post service had barely begun, however, when it was abruptly stopped. A Dutch warship sailed into New York harbor and forced the English authorities to surrender. The Dutch briefly took over their old colony and for the next year New York was New Amsterdam, and the colony of New York became New Netherland.

King Philip escaped after the final battle of King Philip's War in 1675 but was hunted down and killed a year later.

In 1675 when the English took back their colony—and once again changed the Dutch names to English ones—they faced troubles of a different sort. Chief Metacom, the Wampanoag leader whom the English called King Philip, started a war against Massachusetts settlers. King Philip's War disrupted mail service for several more years.

When mail service finally resumed, England's king put it under the control of a private company. He appointed Thomas Neale to run the company, though Neale stayed in England and put his deputy in the colonies in charge. Neale's postal company extended mail service. Many great roads that had been king's highways became post roads. Nearly all had been old Indian paths and most were well-used trails between settlements. A post road from Boston now reached as far north as Portsmouth, New Hampshire. South of New York, a post road served Philadelphia, Pennsylvania and Newcastle, Delaware (just south of Wilmington). The trail along the Hudson River between Albany and New York became a post road, as did Old Connecticut Path from Albany to Springfield.

From Boston three post roads now led to New York. Besides the original Upper Post Road (through Springfield

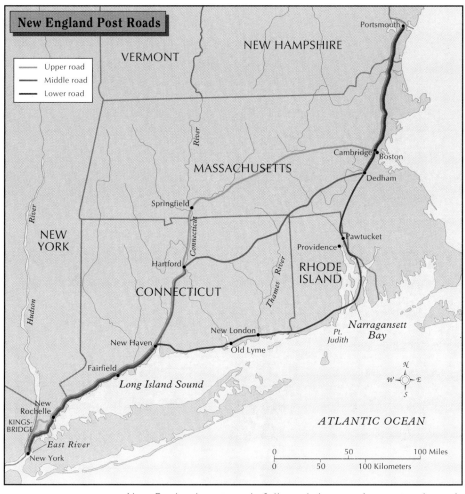

New England post roads followed three major routes through the colonies by the end of the seventeenth century.

and Hartford) there was a Middle Post Road that followed a shortcut from Boston to Hartford, bypassing Springfield. A Lower Post Road followed a coastal route, going south to Providence, then along the Rhode Island and Connecticut coastlines to New York. Although the Lower Post Road was the longest (270 miles), in later years it was the most frequently traveled of the three Boston-New York roads.

Riding with the Postrider

A postrider was required to let travelers accompany him, and to direct them to the best roads and stopping places along the way. In 1704, Boston schoolteacher Sarah Kemble Knight made the journey from New Haven to New York on horseback, riding sidesaddle, in the company of a postrider. Following the Lower Post Road along the coast, Mrs. Knight spent seven days and six nights on the journey. Often her day started at four in the morning. At one inn, she had to sleep on mattresses made of rustling corn husks and share the room with other guests. She found much of the food terrible, the roads worse. She once had to brave the horseback ride over tottering bridges and a narrow path covered with rocks. Another time while crossing a bridge her horse stumbled and Mrs. Knight almost fell into the water. While riding along the coast she and the postrider came

to a hill so steep that they had to walk for a mile, leading their horses. Still, she relished the adventure, for in her day it was unheard of for a woman to travel alone.

Roads made of logs as shown here were known as corduroy roads and made for a very bumpy ride for passengers traveling in early stagecoaches.

By 1706 a postrider made a round-trip eight times a year from Philadelphia to the Potomac River (later the site of Washington, D.C.)—but not necessarily on a regular schedule. He left Philadelphia only when he had enough letters to cover the expenses of his journey.

Later in the 1700s mail service from Boston to Portsmouth, New Hampshire, was extended north to Falmouth (now Portland, Maine). Schedules were kept only when the weather allowed. In winter and early spring it was often easier to send mail from Boston to Falmouth by boat. From there the local post person would try to deliver it by sleigh or on snowshoes.

During the early years of the postal service, laws required every able-bodied New England man between 16 and 60 to spend at least one day a year helping to build and maintain the post roads. Anyone who refused had to pay a fine of five shillings per day—an enormous sum at that time. Still there were seldom enough willing hands to clear the entire post road of tangled brush or fallen branches after a storm. And after a spring thaw, the mud made many of the roads impassable.

At the start of the Revolutionary War, the Americans abandoned the king's postal system and started their own. The Continental Congress appointed Benjamin Franklin the postmaster general. The war changed how mail was delivered. Since British soldiers occupied colonial towns and took over the main post roads to march their armies and haul supplies, postriders switched to new roads and trails to avoid meeting enemy soldiers.

After the war, stagecoaches carried mail for the first time. The advantages of coach delivery were many. The stagecoaches had room to haul more letters and packages, and could protect them from wind, rain, or snow. The mail

Milestones and Other Novelties

In 1751 the king appointed Benjamin Franklin and William Hunter as joint deputy postmasters in the colonies. Hunter was in charge of southern colonies, Franklin handled mail service for northern colonies. In his role as deputy postmaster, Franklin reorganized the system, ending free delivery of newspapers, and streamlining the service. He had the postriders travel night and day on the round-trip between Philadelphia and New York. Later he did the same for riders making round-trips from Philadelphia to Boston. That meant a letter could go to Boston and a reply be returned to Philadelphia in three weeks.

Benjamin Franklin started the use of milestones. At that time, charge for delivering a letter was based on how far the letter was carried. Franklin built a special vehicle to measure distances accurately. With this contraption he traveled along the Boston Post Road. Behind followed men with stones. Each mile, the men marked and placed a stone. Mile markers were placed along other post roads, too. The road from New York to Albany received its red sandstone markers in 1752.

The milestones turned out to be useful in ways other than for calculating postage. They made it easy to identify where along the road something was located. During the Revolutionary War a Continental Army soldier could report on British actions by precise location—for example, "enemy seen collecting grain from every farm as far as the 8th Milestone."

By the mid to end of the eighteenth century the Boston Post Road was well traveled with comfortable inns along the way.

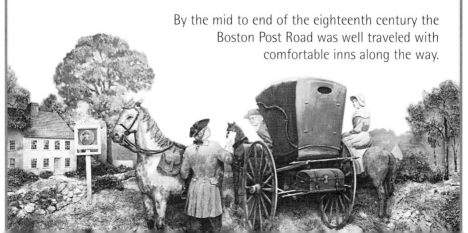

Changing horses for a mail-coach was a typical scene
at inns along the eastern post roads.

was safer, too, since the coaches often carried an armed
guard. Over smaller post roads, however, postriders continued to deliver mail for many more years.

Although the government was slow to build a post road
between Natchez, Mississippi, and Nashville, Tennessee, a
postrider started to carry mail between the two towns in
1798. The rider traveled along the Natchez Trace (see
Chapter 7), an ancient Natchez, Chickasaw, and Choctaw
trail that wound through the wilderness for 500 miles.

By the early 1800s, post roads connected Philadelphia
with the main towns to the south—Baltimore in Maryland,
Wilmington in North Carolina, and Savannah in Georgia.
In 1819, the United States bought Florida from Spain and
the new nation's coastal post road extended from northern
Maine to Jacksonville, Florida. By this time, stagecoaches
carried nearly all of the mail. No longer did the lone
postrider, tin trumpet at the ready, sweep across the land
with the king's post. Now it was a horse-drawn coach that
rumbled into town as its driver announced—with a blast of
his brass horn—the arrival of the U.S. Mail.

THREE

Battle Trails:
Nemacolin's Path (Washington's Road), Braddock's Road, and the Forbes Road

Nemacolin's Path (Washington's Road)

In 1748, young George Washington—not yet 20—and his half brother Lawrence helped a group of Virginia colonists form the Ohio Company. Its goal was to establish fur trade with the Native Americans and start settlements in the upper valley of the Ohio River—now eastern Ohio and western Pennsylvania. The company hired frontiersman Christopher Gist to survey the area, and to find the shortest portage (overland route) between the Potomac River and the Monongahela, one of the rivers that join the Ohio at what is now Pittsburgh.

Part of the way Christopher Gist followed old east-west Indian trading paths that began in Virginia and Maryland. From the Ohio Company's storehouse on Wills Creek near present-day Cumberland, Maryland, Gist angled northwest. He crossed mountains and valleys until he reached the Monongahela River at what is now Brownsville, Pennsylvania. Today's highway U.S. 40 roughly parallels the path Gist followed.

After Gist made his survey the Ohio Company asked Nemacolin, son of a Delaware chief, to help blaze a trail over Gist's route. The new trail, made wide enough to allow packhorses to pass, was called Nemacolin's Path.

At this time both England and France laid claim to the land along the Ohio River—the English because it was part of Virginia's original land grants in 1609, and the French because of La Salle's visit there in 1669. To back their claim the French built a string of forts in the valley. The English sprang into action. They knew that once the French controlled the Ohio River valley, English settlers could never settle there, and would have to remain in their colonies east of the Appalachians.

At 21, George Washington became a major in the Virginia Militia, a volunteer army, and was sent by Virginia's governor to deliver a letter to the French in the Ohio Valley. It warned the French that they were trespassing on Virginia territory and requested that they leave.

Washington hired his old fencing tutor Jacob van Braam as interpreter for the expedition to the French forts. He also took along two hunters, two Indian traders, and Mr. Gist as guide. The men left on horseback from the Ohio Company

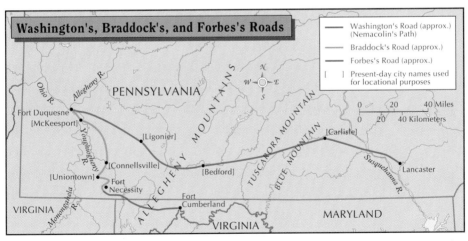

Three early trails in western Pennsylvania were established in the mid-to-late-seventeenth century so that British troops could reach and combat French strongholds in the area.

storehouse on Wills Creek in mid-November, 1753. Following Nemacolin's Path, they spent a week plowing their way through rain and snow to the Monongahela River. From there they continued downriver to "the forks," where the Monongahela, Ohio, and Allegheny Rivers meet—now the city of Pittsburgh. Washington noted that the forks would make an excellent site for an English fort.

When the men reached the first of the new French strongholds, the commanding officer was away. They went on to the second, where the French officer received Washington with courtesy. His answer to the Virginia governor's letter was polite but firm: the French had plans to occupy the Ohio Valley, and they intended to do so!

Washington and his men had no choice but to return to Virginia. The trip back was a miserable experience that included being fired at by Indians. Later as they floated down the Allegheny on a raft, Washington was knocked into the ice-filled stream and nearly drowned.

Virginia's Governor Dinwiddie's response to the French officer's defiant reply was immediate. He sent a group of workers to build a fort at the forks, in the middle of the so-called "French territory." Before the men could finish their job, French soldiers arrived. The soldiers sent the workers away, destroyed the half-finished building, and in its place put up a fort of their own. They called it Fort Duquesne.

To Governor Dinwiddie, this was an act of war. He promoted George Washington to lieutenant colonel and once more sent him west—this time with a regiment of the Virginia Militia to halt the French advance. Again Washington followed Nemacolin's Path from Wills Creek. He had his men level the path and clear away bushes and underbrush so the swivel guns (small cannon) and supply wagons could get through. What had been "Nemacolin's

George Washington (center) holds a night council with his officers at Fort Necessity.

Path" soon became known as "Washington's Road."

On a marshy creek bottom a few miles southeast of present-day Uniontown, Pennsylvania, Washington's men dug a trench and put up a temporary fort. Then scouts moved forward to search for the enemy. They met a small number of French soldiers and after a brief skirmish drove them off. The Virginians returned to their temporary fort and built a stronger one—called Fort Necessity. Then they waited. The French attack came a few days later. Through a heavy rain 500 French soldiers charged from the forest, guns blazing as they shot at the defenders of Fort Necessity, and even at the Virginia militiamen's cows and dogs.

The rain kept falling, turning the trenches of Fort Necessity into soft mud. Water soaked ammunition boxes and left the Virginians' muskets and cannons useless. Instead of Washington stopping the French, the French stopped him. At day's end, George Washington surrendered. Since the Indian allies of the French had killed all of the Virginians' horses, Washington and his men had to walk back to Fort Cumberland on Wills Creek. With that battle, the French and Indian War began.

Braddock's Road and the Forbes Road

A year later, in 1754, England's king chose Major General Edward Braddock to attempt what Washington had failed to do—take Fort Duquesne. Once the general captured that French stronghold, he was to lead his troops north to capture France's Fort Niagara on Lake Ontario.

From England, General Braddock brought recruits. When these soldiers arrived in Virginia's port of Alexandria, Braddock combined them with militiamen from New York, Virginia, Maryland, and North and South Carolina. Few Pennsylvanians had volunteered to fight the battle. The mostly-Quaker settlers of that colony did not believe in war.

General Braddock appointed George Washington his aide, or personal assistant, and began to collect the money, wagons, horses, and provisions he would need for the march west to Fort Duquesne. General Braddock intended to follow Washington's Road (the widened Nemacolin's Path) from Fort Cumberland—but not as Washington had left it. Instead, the English general insisted on improving the road. He wanted it 12 feet wide to allow room for his many supply wagons and heavy cannons.

Braddock sent an army of 600 woodchoppers scurrying ahead of nearly 1,000 marching soldiers. While the battalion of axmen felled trees, leveled rough spots in the road, and even put up bridges the soldiers had to wait. This annoyed Washington, anxious to move on. Besides the time lost on road-building, Braddock had other problems. Supply wagons broke down, or became stuck in the bogs.

Many wagons had to be abandoned when the horses pulling them died or were injured and had to be killed. On steep inclines, men often had to lower the overloaded wagons with rope and tackle. Then the men had to help the exhausted horses pull the wagons up to the next ridge. In this way, it took the general over a month to get from Fort Cumberland to the Monongahela River. On some days he gained fewer than two miles.

On July 7, 1755, the soldiers neared the river, and were only a dozen miles from Fort Duquesne. Braddock hurried ahead with a "flying column" of 1,459 of his finest men. Flag bearers waved their flags. Drummers beat their drums. Soldier musicians played "The Grenadiers' March" on their fifes. And English soldiers in scarlet coats and the blue-coated colonial militiamen and officers on their horses splashed through the shallow Monongahela. Horse-drawn cannons and supply wagons followed. As soon as the last wagon was across the river, French and Indian sharp-shooters—hidden behind trees and in ravines—began firing rifles. The English panicked. At the head of the line, marching in close formation, the soldiers in their scarlet and blue coats were easy targets. And surrounded by an enemy they couldn't see, they couldn't fight back.

Although Braddock tried to rally his men, it was hopeless. Washington had two horses shot out from under him, General Braddock even more. The fight was soon over. Soldiers carried Braddock, shot in the lungs and dying, back across the river with the retreating army. He lost 977 men, while only 25 French soldiers had been killed. As the remnants of the army staggered back to Fort Cumberland over Braddock's Road, officers ordered that the stores and provisions be destroyed so the few wagons still usable could carry the wounded.

In this painting by Edwin Willard Deming of Braddock's defeat, the general is shown at the moment he was shot from his horse by French and Indian sharpshooters.

After the defeat at the Monongahela, the British abandoned Fort Cumberland. Braddock's Road was soon overgrown with brush and trees, to be used only by a few British scouts and Native Americans.

Three years later, the English made a third try to take Fort Duquesne, with General John Forbes in charge. Forbes considered marching his men over Braddock's Road, then decided to create a new road. He chose a route north of Braddock's, but in case he needed a backup route, Forbes had his men clear parts of Braddock's Road as well.

The new road started near Lancaster, Pennsylvania. Unlike Braddock's Road, this one was narrow and winding as it followed closely two Indian trading trails—the

Kittanning and the Highland. The east-west road passed through the present Pennsylvania towns of Carlisle, Bedford, and Ligonier.

On this third try to oust the French from Fort Duquesne, the English succeeded. As General Forbes and his army stormed the French stronghold, French soldiers scattered. The English moved into the fort and changed its name to Fort Pitt in honor of the British statesman William Pitt. The town that grew up around the fort was first called Pittsborough, and later Pittsburgh.

The French and Indian War lasted until 1763. Even before the English finally won that long struggle, colonists from Virginia and Maryland and other parts of the east had started to move west to settle along the Ohio River valley. They usually came by way of Fort Pitt—"the gateway to the west." The commander of Fort Pitt tried to stop the flow of emigrants. He even issued a proclamation that these western lands were to be set aside for the Indians as a hunting ground. Since there was no way to enforce the ruling, these early settlers ignored it and kept on coming. Most

Colonel George Washington (center) raises his hat to salute the British flag flying over Fort Pitt (formerly Fort Duquesne) in 1758 after the British defeated the French.

reached their new homes west of the Allegheny and Appalachian Mountains by way of the roads General Braddock and General Forbes had built.

A Failed Attack on Quebec

An important early trail south from Quebec in Canada led to the mouth of the Kennebec River on the coast of Maine—in colonial times a part of Massachusetts. At the start of the Revolutionary War, Congress sent Benedict Arnold north through Maine to occupy Quebec, a fortified town held by the French, and thus conquer all of Canada. With 500 soldiers Arnold followed the Quebec Trail, going part of the way by boats—which they had to build—and then by portage from the Kennebec River to Dead River, and to the Chain of Ponds, and finally to the shores of the St. Lawrence River opposite Quebec City. There they attacked Quebec on New Year's Eve, 1775, but the attack failed and they were forced to return along the same route—which came to be known as the Arnold Trail.

This early view of Quebec in 1758 shows the upper town with its church and convent spires, the lower town near the St. Lawrence River, and in the foreground, across the river, the town now called Lévis.

FOUR

Emigrant Trails
and Freight Roads

Pennsylvania

P hiladelphia was a favorite port in the early 1700s for newcomers arriving from Europe by ship. Many German-speaking emigrants from Germany and Switzerland settled farther west in Lancaster and nearby counties. They came to be called "Pennsylvania Dutch" because they spoke a mixture of their native tongue and English. (In German, the word for "German" is *Deutsch*.) The new emigrants became farmers, coopers (barrel-makers), or craftspersons, or they worked at iron planta-

Philadelphia in the eighteenth century, depicted in this lithograph of 1875, appeared to be a crowded and busy place as seen from across the Delaware River in New Jersey.

45

tions—places where pig iron (crude iron before refining) was made. To get their corn, woven and leather goods, wood carvings, and iron, to market the settlers loaded them onto packhorses. Then two or three men would tie the head of one horse to the tail of the horse in front and lead the string of 12 or 15 horses single file along the narrow path eastward to Philadelphia.

The path from Lancaster, once an Indian trail, was rocky and full of stumps. There were no bridges over streams. Since the packhorses could travel only about 15 miles in a day, the 70-mile journey took several days. As more people and pack animals used the trail it was widened and

Beyond the Alleghenies

For settlers who lived beyond the Allegheny Mountains in the valley of the Monongahela River in the late 1700s, Philadelphia was too far away for trade. Instead, these backcountry folk sent their skins and pelts, corn whiskey, grain, poultry, butter, and other products by packtrain to closer towns—Morgantown in what is now West Virginia, and Baltimore, Frederick, and Fort Cumberland in Maryland. In these larger trade centers, they bartered their goods for needed gunpowder, spices, salt, iron, or manufactured articles. Like the other settlers who sent packtrains to market, families in the backcountry chose a master driver and one or two helpers to haul everyone's goods. Bells around the horses' necks warned the drivers if the animals strayed at night. At the start of the journey, the men brought bags of corn, which they left at various places along the trail, to feed the horses on the return trip. For themselves, the men carried wallets (leather lunch boxes) with bread, beef jerky, boiled ham, and cheese. They hoped to find game to shoot when that ran out.

The Conestoga Wagon

The Conestoga wagons with their wide, heavy wheels originated in Pennsylvania in the early 1700s. Soon they became the most popular means of hauling freight in other states, too. The wagon had an unusual curved body, a foot higher at each end to keep goods from falling out on hills, and help the wagon float across deep streams. The Conestoga's underbody was always painted blue. The upper woodwork was bright red. Hoops along the center of the wagon held a canvas cover to protect freight from the weather. The curved cover, bleached white in the sun, gave the effect of a great ship swaying up and down the billowy hills. Later pioneers who drove Conestogas across the plains west of the Mississippi called them "prairie schooners."

Usually a team of five or six horses, bells on their collars, drew the Contestoga wagon. The heyday of the Conestoga was around 1815, but some were in use as late as 1860.

A typical Conestoga wagon, on display at the Shelburne Museum in Shelburne, Vermont, provided the basic means of transportation for family migrations to new homesteads in the West.

improved to become a road. People heading east called it the Philadelphia Road. Those going the other way called it the Lancaster Road.

Once the counties near Philadelphia and Lancaster became crowded with settlers, new emigrants from Europe had to go even farther west to find farmland. Many of these later settlers—mostly Scotch-Irish—crossed the Susquehanna River to York and Cumberland Counties. They, too, used packtrains to get their goods to market, following the Kittanning and other Indian trails eastward until they reached the Philadelphia Road at Lancaster.

Gradually, horse-drawn freight carts replaced many of the packtrains on the Philadelphia-Lancaster Road. These carts had wheels of solid wood, cut from the end of large logs. By the mid-1700s, bright red and blue Conestoga wagons with white canvas covers began to appear. Their name came from the small village in southeastern Pennsylvania where they were built. The Conestoga wagons soon became the most popular way to transport goods both to and from Philadelphia.

Freight wagons going into the city might haul anything from wheat, leather saddles, and lumber to whiskey, flour,

A winter scene on the Lancaster - Philadelphia road in 1795 shows a coach full of passengers being passed by a Conestoga wagon. The custom of driving on the right supposedly was started by Conestoga wagon drivers.

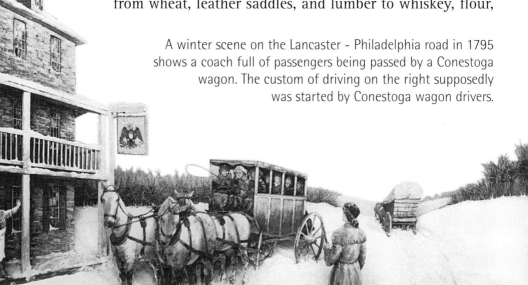

Early Iron Production

Many of the freight wagons rumbling between Lancaster and Philadelphia hauled iron for export to England, or to be used locally by blacksmiths for making nails, tools, and other iron products. Iron plantations operated in many parts of central and southern Pennsylvania. Workers mixed iron ore dug from the ground, with limestone and melted it over burning charcoal in a blast furnace. Then they poured the molten iron into rectangular-shaped hollows in sand or clay to form crude iron bars called "pigs." At a nearby forge, workers reheated and hammered the "pigs" into thin strips or bars for blacksmiths and toolmakers to use. This was the start of Pennsylvania's iron and steel industries.

and flax. Those going west might carry manufactured items or the household goods of emigrant families moving to the frontier. At first, the west-bound wagons went only as far as Lancaster. Year by year the road to the west improved until it finally reached Carlisle. Eventually, a good road led all the way to Pittsburgh.

In the late 1700s traffic jammed the Lancaster-Philadelphia Road. Conestoga wagons jostled with pack-trains, stagecoaches, and small farm wagons for space. Farmers or hired drovers brought their cattle or hogs to market along the main road. And more inns lined the road, offering meals or overnight accommodations.

Ohio

At the same time the first pioneers were settling the region around Philadelphia in the early 1700s, far to the west the French were trying to keep settlers away from the valleys of the Mississippi and Ohio Rivers and land around the Great Lakes. The French and Indian War settled the dispute over who controlled this territory, and the peace treaty of 1763 gave the land to the English. Right away, large numbers of non-French emigrant families began to move west into the Ohio Valley.

Among these early settlers was Ebenezer Zane. He followed the Braddock Road west from Virginia to establish what is now Wheeling, West Virginia, on the Ohio River about 50 miles southwest of Pittsburgh. More pioneer settlers arrived after the Revolutionary War. Some had just arrived from Europe, while others had lived for a time in the colonies. Most of the former colonists were shopkeepers and craftspersons who lost their businesses during the war, poor farmers, or veterans anxious to make a fresh start.

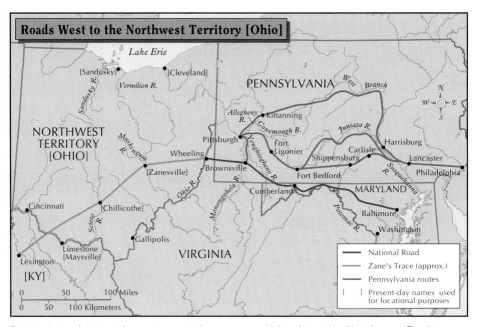

By the late eighteenth century settlers were pushing into the Northwest Territory (Ohio) along routes in Maryland and Pennsylvania.

With the Northwest Ordinance of 1787, Congress gave its approval for people to settle in Northwest Territory— land between what was then the nation's western frontier and the Mississippi River. According to the ordinance, as soon as 60,000 free male inhabitants (the only people eligible to vote) occupied one section of the Northwest Territory, that section could become a state.

Soon after the Northwest Ordinance was adopted, a group of war veterans in New England, calling themselves the Ohio Company of Associates, signed a contract with the government to buy one and a half million acres of land along the north bank of the Ohio River in what is now southeastern Ohio. In December, 22 members of the company headed west from Ipswich, Massachusetts, to start a settlement.

In their ox-drawn wagon the young pioneers carried tools to build the boats to travel on western Pennsylvania's rivers once the overland trails ended. On the canvas cover of the wagon was painted the message: FOR THE OHIO COUNTRY. Striding beside the wagon, the men followed roads where they could, and blazed their own paths when necessary. Their route took them from Boston to Springfield, across a corner of Connecticut, and into southern New York. At Newburgh, they crossed the Hudson River by ferryboat. From New York State they cut through the northwest corner of New Jersey.

Once they reached Harrisburg, Pennsylvania, the pioneers bound for their "Ohio Country" followed trails and roads that had long since replaced the old Forbes Road. Early in January of 1788 they reached Simeral's Ferry (now West Newton), on the Youghiogheny River 30 miles southeast of Pittsburgh. It had been almost eight weeks since they left home.

Immediately the carpenters set to work building dugout canoes and two large flatboats. Soon 26 more members of their company arrived to help finish the job. This second group had started later from Hartford, Connecticut, and had run into trouble when deep snow forced them to give up wagon travel and make sleds to haul their goods.

Once the boats were ready, the pioneers gathered provisions—including flour and meat as well as a ton of hay to feed the horses and oxen—and started downriver. They floated along the Youghiogheny to the Monongahela. They left that river at the forks in Pittsburgh to float on the Ohio River down to the Muskingum River. Near a military post on the banks of the Ohio, they came ashore to found the Marietta colony, Ohio's first permanent settlement.

Settlers in other parts of the northwest took similar routes from the east, following land trails for the first part of their journey west, and then changing to "water trails" for the last part. They settled river towns, such as Cincinnati and Gallipolis, and founded settlements farther inland, such as Chillicothe. To make it easier for settlers scattered throughout the northwest to communicate with one another, the government gave land to men willing to open new trails and ferry services.

Ebenezer Zane, founder of the river port of Wheeling, was among those who accepted the government's offer. In 1796, with his brother and his son-in-law, Zane created a trail that cut across what is now southeastern Ohio. Much of the way Zane followed an old Indian trail, overgrown with small trees and bushes. It took the men about eight months to clear the underbrush from the path and install ferries at some of the streams too deep to ford. Besides the land payment, Zane was given the right to operate these ferries. Zane's Trace—soon used by postriders as well as

Flat rafts, such as this ferry pulled along a rope, were often the means of crossing a river for early travelers along the trails.

settlers—went from Wheeling through what became the Ohio towns of Zanesville, Lancaster, and Chillicothe to Limestone (later Maysville) in Kentucky, 226 miles to the southwest. Beyond Limestone a path along an ancient buffalo route already led to Lexington and other early Kentucky settlements.

By 1803 Ohio had a population large enough for it to be admitted to the Union as a state. Later other sections of the Northwest Territory became the states of Michigan, Indiana, Illinois, and Wisconsin.

FIVE

Another Trail West: Boone's Wilderness Road

Frontiersman Daniel Boone was a private in a North Carolina county militia when the French and Indian War began. He joined General Braddock's forces as a teamster (wagon driver), and was driving a supply wagon the day of Braddock's disastrous defeat at the Monongahela. As the battle raged, the teamsters were ordered to hold their horses at the ready, for the advance. Only there was no advance. Instead it was a rout, as the few British troops to survive the slaughter turned and ran for the river with the enemy in hot pursuit. Many teamsters cut loose their horses and fled. Boone waited for a time, but when French Canadian soldiers and their Indian allies closed in, he, too, slashed the harness, leaped onto the lead horse, and raced for the river.

Within the year, Boone's life became more peaceful. He was living in the backwoods of North Carolina, married to his sweetheart Rebecca, and doing what he loved best—shooting and trapping game. By the 1760s, he had become a "long hunter," going on hunting trips that lasted for many months. He wandered through the wilderness north and west of his farm, including parts of Kentucky. He had first heard about Kentucky, favorite hunting ground of the Shawnee and the Cherokee, from John Findley, a fellow wagon driver for General Braddock.

Boone was an able trail-maker, hunter, and trapper. He had the patience to lie in wait for hours until deer or other animals came to a salt lick—a place near salt springs—to lick the dried salt ponds or salt-encrusted earth and rocks. After a successful season Boone often brought home hundreds of deer, beaver, and otter skins to sell. He killed bears, too. He might note the event by carving on a tree, although the words were likely to be "cilled a bar." Daniel Boone could read and write, but was a dreadful speller!

By chance, in 1769, Boone ran into his wartime friend John Findley, now a horse trader and backcountry peddler. Again the two talked about Kentucky—especially the interior that Boone had not seen. Findley called it a paradise for hunters—with deer at every salt lick, buffalo on every trail, wild geese and ducks galore, and Native Americans with plenty of pelts to trade. Findley proposed to Boone that they explore Kentucky together, so they organized an expedition with Boone's brother-in-law, John Stewart, and three others. Findley felt there was a better way to reach the interior than the way Boone had wandered across the mountains into eastern Kentucky. He suggested that they cross into Kentucky farther south, on the Great Warrior's Path of the Cherokee. And so they did, passing through the V-shaped notch in the mountains known as

Daniel Boone with his long rifle and coonskin cap on the trail.

Cumberland Gap. A colonist from Virginia, Dr. Thomas Walker, had named this gap for England's Duke of Cumberland while exploring this area in 1750.

Despite being captured by the Shawnee a couple of times, Boone had such a good time hunting and trapping that he and Stewart stayed in Kentucky long after Findley and the others gave up on the adventure and left. Even after Stewart disappeared, apparently killed by Indians, Boone remained in Kentucky and did not leave for two years. From time to time his brother Squire brought essentials, such as ammunition, flour, and salt. On each visit, Squire took home Daniel's collection of furs to sell.

A year after Daniel Boone finally returned to his North Carolina farm, he was back in eastern Kentucky to hunt and explore. This time he met two surveyors, and saw

Boone's First Try

Two years before he led the first emigrants through the Cumberland Gap into central Kentucky in 1775, Daniel Boone had tried to settle his wife, Rebecca, and their children in eastern Kentucky—legally the land of the Cherokee and the Shawnee. About a dozen families besides the Boones made the attempt. The trail they followed was the path Boone had taken on his first hunting trips into eastern Kentucky. It was too rough for wagons, so the people packed tools, clothing, and treasured possessions on horses. The small childen rode in baskets tied to ropes slung across the animals' backs. The settlers carried their chickens the same way, and drove their cattle and hogs single file along the trail. After Indians attacked, killing several adults and children including Boone's son, the discouraged families gave up and trekked back to North Carolina.

other surveyors' red flags marking off parcels of land. He realized it would not be long before Kentucky was settled. Richard Henderson, a North Carolina lawyer, felt the same. The two knew one another, and in 1774 Henderson hired the frontiersman to help assemble the Cherokee for a meeting to discuss selling their land.

Although private individuals were not allowed to buy land from the Indians, Richard Henderson met with Cherokee chiefs to trade for a huge tract that included almost all of Kentucky and much of Tennessee. He offered the Indians six wagonloads of merchandise—sacks of corn, flour, blankets, guns, powder, lead, casks of rum, and various trinkets and other goods—and the Cherokee accepted.

With lawyers representing the Cherokee, both buyer and seller signed a treaty in March 1775. Next, Henderson put out a call for settlers. In newspaper advertisements he offered free land to those willing to grow large crops of corn or raise flocks of sheep. Then he sent Daniel Boone and 30 armed men on horseback to blaze a trail wide and level enough for settlers' wagons to reach the region around present-day Lexington, Kentucky. That was where Henderson planned to put his capital.

Boone blazed his trail from Long Island, a settlement on the Holston River in the southwest tip of Virginia. Most of the road builders were Boone's friends and relatives. To cook and run the camp, two women went along—a slave woman and Boone's daughter Susannah, whose husband was one of the road crew. While leading the way, Boone hunted game for each evening's meal.

Daniel Boone led the group through the southwestern corner of Virginia. As the men pushed through the forest and went up mountains and along river valleys, they had to hack at vines and overhanging branches, chop down

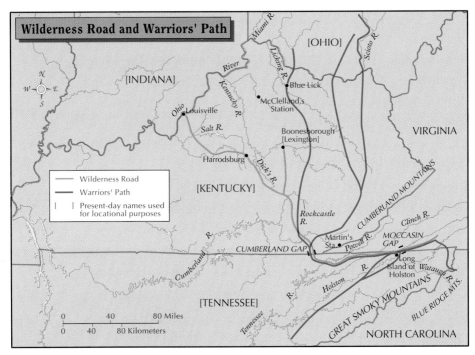

Mid-to-late-eighteenth century trails from southern
Virginia into Kentucky and Tennessee.

saplings, and cut through dense growths of tall, woody
grasses. They followed the Powell valley south, continuing
alongside the high peaks of the Cumberland Mountains
until they were within about 25 miles of Cumberland Gap.
Here the trail narrowed, for to make it wide enough for
wagons had become almost impossible.

The crossing at Cumberland Gap was not difficult.
Migrating buffalo, deer, and other animals in search of
food had long tramped through this natural doorway.
Native Americans learned about the gap as they followed
the animal trails, and it became their main pass through
the mountains to the hunting grounds. Indian warriors and
traders who came south from the Potomac River crossed
the Cumberlands here before turning north to the Ohio River.

Beyond Cumberland Gap, Boone followed the so-called Warriors' Path for about 25 miles, then left it to follow the same buffalo trace, or path, that he took when he hunted there five years before. On that trip, Daniel Boone had come to know the territory well, but blazing a trail settlers would follow presented a greater challenge. Among the settlers would be women and children, horses loaded with supplies, and dogs and sheep. Boone had to find low mountain passes and streams that could be easily forded. Often that meant meandering along creeks, or crossing the same creek many times.

As Daniel Boone and his trail builders moved north into the interior of Kentucky, they were on constant lookout for angry Shawnee or others who might attack. Not every Native American here liked the idea that his favorite hunting ground had been sold by the Cherokee to Henderson for settlement. Thus far, the trail makers met no Indians, but soon after they came down from the hills onto the plains of

An engraving of the Cumberland Gap as seen from Eagle Cliff.

Kentucky in what is now Madison County, a war party of Shawnee attacked Boone's camp and killed several men. Boone refused to let this hold him back and he sent a letter to Henderson, saying he didn't think they should let the Indians stop them from settling the area.

Near what is now Lexington, Kentucky, Daniel Boone built a fort and started a settlement he called Boonesborough. By this time, Henderson was already leading the first group of settlers along the newly-blazed trail that people called Boone's Trace. When Henderson received Boone's letter about the Indian attack, some settlers turned around immediately and headed for home. Others, though frightened, kept going.

In the valley of the Powell River where Boone's Trace became narrower, John Martin operated a pioneer outpost called Martin's Station. Here Henderson's group of settlers had a chance to rest, stock up on provisions, and transfer their goods from wagons to pack animals. They had to leave some of their bags of salt, as there was no space in the packs to haul all of them. As a result, the settlers had run out of this vital seasoning and preservative by the time Daniel Boone left Boonesborough later in the year to bring back his family and a second group of settlers. So Boone took several young men from the new settlement with him as far as Martin's Station to collect the bags of salt that had been left behind.

Daniel Boone in brown coat and red scarf is shown leading a group of settlers through the Cumberland Gap in this painting by George Caleb Bingham.

Traveling in Groups

Once settlements were established in the interior of Kentucky in the late 1700s, people began to travel both directions along the Wilderness Road. Because of the constant risk of an Indian attack, and for a safer journey, travelers formed companies. A company in the east or south preparing to leave for Kentucky would advertise in local papers for other families who wanted to go along, as would Kentucky companies starting down the Wilderness Road toward Virginia and points east and south. From Kentucky there were usually two or three departures a month.

Although there were perils along the trail that Henderson described as "hilly, stony, slippery, and miry," settlers kept coming west over Boone's Trace. By the end of the Revolutionary War about 12,000 persons followed this wilderness trail to the new territory. By 1800, the total was 300,000. Among the early pioneers who crossed into Kentucky over Boone's Trace—later called the Wilderness Road—was Abraham Hanks, whose daughter Nancy was to become the mother of Abraham Lincoln.

As the years went by, settlements sprang up along the Wilderness Road. Besides Martin's Station, other stations (innkeepers' cabins) were built where families could get food, lodging, and provisions including seed corn and "Irish taters" to plant on their new farms. On their way west on the trail the early pioneers also stopped at mills for flour.

Once settled, farmers from Kentucky began to drive thousands of sheep and cattle to eastern markets every year along the Wilderness Road. It remained an important trail until the early 1800s.

SIX

Toll Roads and Turnpikes

By the late 1700s, the once narrow footpath between Lancaster and Philadelphia had become a bustling two-way road with traffic problems. The need for a better, safer road was obvious. So Pennsylvania lawmakers granted a charter to the Philadelphia and Lancaster Turnpike Road Company to build such a road. To pay building costs, officials of the road company sold shares in their company to investors. When the new road was finished users would have to pay a fee. These fees would give the road company enough money to pay back each shareholder's original investment, and also maintain the road. To collect the fees, a tollgate was to be placed every few miles. The gatekeeper would drop the gate—a long pole with sharp spikes, or pikes—to close the road until a user, such as a drover with a flock of sheep or a wagon driver, paid the toll. Then the gatekeeper would turn the piked pole out of the way and let the traveler continue on the "turnpike," as the toll road came to be called, until the next tollgate.

Workers began to build the turnpike between Lancaster and Philadelphia in 1792. They finished two years later, at a cost of nearly half a million dollars. From the start, this first turnpike made a great deal of money for its investors. Other companies throughout the East rushed to build turnpikes. Soon there were turnpikes leading into Baltimore, in both the Carolinas, and between Hartford and New Haven. The old Mohegan Trail of the Connecticut Indians was made into a turnpike from Norwich to New London. In New York the Iroquois war trail over the flat Lake Ontario Plain became the turnpike between Syracuse and Watertown. Two other two turnpikes led west from Albany to Lake Erie–the Mohawk Route (more or less the route of today's Interstate 90) and the Great Western Turnpike (present U.S. 20). Over these turnpikes farmers in western New York hauled wheat to eastern markets and drovers herded beef cattle to slaughterhouses.

The rules for building new turnpikes in New York were typical–and specific. The road had to be raised in the middle so water flowed off at the sides. Workers had to use durable timber for bridges and a bridge had to be three feet above the water at the water's greatest height.

Instead of building new roads, some companies improved existing roads and called them turnpikes. "Improved" meant anything from a new rock and gravel surface to simply taking away a few boulders and topping boggy places with gravel. Some turnpikes were dirt roads or corduroy roads– made by placing logs close together and half-covering them with dirt– but most were paved with small broken stones, the best road surface for every season of the year.

From the late 1700s through the first decades of the next century turnpikes were popular. People moved around more easily. Turnpikes were the roads of choice for stagecoaches, Conestoga freight wagons, riders on horseback, drovers, tin peddlers with small wagons full of small useful items, and emigrants moving west in covered wagons.

Turnpike charges varied, but at each tollgate the fee was around one penny (equal to about 30 cents today) for

Tolls collected at a tollgate, such as this one on the Maysville Turnpike in Kentucky, helped to provide for the maintenance of privately owned roads.

every horse, mule, or cow, while sheep and pigs were three cents a dozen. A man riding or leading a horse was charged around four cents. A cart drawn by a pair of oxen cost ten cents, while a wagon and two horses cost twelve and a half cents, the same as it cost in the wintery north for a sled and horses. Fee for a coach or carriage drawn by two horses was twenty-five cents. In most states, the gate-keeper did not collect tolls from persons going to or from church, from people taking their grain to grind at a mill, or from members of the militia.

Human Muscle Power

Since turnpike builders in the 1790s and after had no tractors, bulldozers, or road graders, they depended on the muscle power of men and oxen.

The building of the Lancaster Turnpike was typical. The first stage was to plow the earth, digging out and rolling to the side any large boulders. Then the oxen were used to pull a thick beam over the plowed earth to move loose dirt from the sides to build up the center. To smooth the surface, the animals pulled over it a stone drag—a sort of wooden leveling box weighted with a heavy stone. On steep hills, workers built ridges across the road to divert rainwater to ditches along the sides. Before the builders were finished, they erected tollhouses every ten miles or so. The last stage in the building of the turnpike was to pave the entire road with broken stone.

Later, both turnpikes and the National Road (built in the 1850s) were paved with broken stone called macadam—after the Scottish engineer John L. McAdam, who developed the method. For macadamized roads, limestone was broken into small pieces that fit together to form a solid, hard surface. Gangs of Irish laborers earned six dollars a month for working beside the road breaking the limestone into three-inch pieces with a round-headed hammer. To protect their eyes they wore metal goggles with slits.

A road builder is shown here using an early leveler to take some of the rough bumps out of a road.

Because of heavy use of the turnpikes, upkeep was costly. The owners did not make much money—especially since some people used the turnpikes without paying. Although Americans liked the novelty of the turnpike at first, many soon decided it was silly to pay to travel over roads that were often poorly maintained. So they bypassed the gatekeeper and took what they called the "shunpike"—a pathway that led around the tollhouse.

By the early 1800s, poor profits convinced most turnpike companies to get out of the business and turn their roads over to the states. As the turnpike era came to an end, many farmers and factories found a new way to haul produce to market and distribute manufactured goods. The new way was another kind of "water trail"—the canal.

SEVEN

The Long Trail Home: Natchez Trace

From the late 1700s into the early 1800s, veterans of the Revolutionary War and other easterners swarmed to farmland in the "west"—now the Monongahela and Ohio River valleys in western Pennsylvania, Ohio, Indiana, and Kentucky. The easiest way for these farmers to send produce to market was to float it downstream on flatboats to the Mississippi River, then on south to New Orleans to be loaded onto oceangoing vessels. Some Mississippi flatboats were rough log rafts. Others were finished barges or

An engraving after a painting by George Caleb Bingham shows a group of merrymakers aboard a flatboat like those often seen on the rivers of the Midwest.

Abe Lincoln's Father

In 1806 Abraham Lincoln's father, Thomas, was among those who floated merchandise down the Ohio and the Mississippi in a flatboat and returned by foot on the Natchez Trace.

Twenty-two years later, young Abraham the son made a similar trip. But instead of walking back, he rode on a steamboat.

keelboats. A farmer might float his own goods downstream, or hire someone with a flatboat to take it south. Flatboat cargoes included barrels and bags of tobacco, pork, flour, and grain, and also millstones, animal furs, iron, whiskey, and brandy. Poling a boat upstream was almost impossible, so at the end of the trip most owners sold not only their goods, but also their flatboats, for scrap lumber. Then—pockets full of cash—they headed for home.

For most boatmen, the common way to go north was along the Natchez Trace—once a series of Native American trails between the river town of Natchez in what is now the state of Mississippi, and Nashville, in Tennessee. Unfortunately, by the early 1800s the Trace had become a favorite gathering place for highwaymen. They roamed the area because most travelers on the trail had a lot of money. All these robbers had to do was hide somewhere along the trail—and wait.

One of the most notorious of the outlaws was Samuel Mason, a soldier in the Revolutionary War before he turned to a life of crime. On the dark and gloomy Natchez Trace, he relieved travelers of their horses, watches, gold pieces, silver dollars, and—sometimes—their lives. Mason was a tall man, portly and inclined to swagger. His most unnerving feature was a protruding front tooth which stuck out like a wolf's fang when he became angry. One member of Mason's gang was the equally notorious outlaw Wiley Harpe, known as "Little Harpe." Mason also had a shop-keeper friend in Natchez who stored or sold the gang's loot. The shopkeeper made sure to inform Mason if an especially rich customer was headed for the Trace.

The journey on foot along the 500-mile trail from Natchez to Nashville could take weeks. A faster and more comfortable way to travel the Natchez Trace was on horse-back. Some who followed the trail rode horses they had brought from home on their flatboats. Others bought ani-mals in Natchez, where a horse cost about $50. Often, two men shared a single horse or mule. The procedure was

Jackson and His Bride on the Trace

In 1791 Andrew Jackson went up the Trace with his new bride, Rachel. Both were excellent riders and accustomed to the wilderness. Even so, they wisely traveled in the company of dozens of other people including servants to handle the baggage, prepare meals, and pitch the tents at night.

During the War of 1812 Jackson led his troops on the Trace. The men compared his stamina to the strong and tough hickory trees along the way—and gave Andrew Jackson the nickname "Old Hickory."

A portrait of Andrew Jackson sent to a friend and dated May 1, 1815.

The Natchez Trace as it appears today.

simple. One man started to walk while the other rode. After the rider went a certain distance, he tied up the animal and began to walk. When the first walker reached the horse, he untied it and rode until he caught up with his companion. Again they switched places, continuing to "tie and ride" all the way north to Nashville.

Even after the worst of the bandits on the Trace was arrested and disposed of, there were other hazards on the trail. So those using it generally traveled in groups for protection and company. The long trail wound through thick brush and forests of oak and pine and hickory. It passed through open country and across dismal swamps. In the swamps, the swarms of gnats and mosquitoes were an irritation, but the real danger was losing the trail completely. Sixty miles northeast of Natchez marked the dividing line between the settled part of Mississippi and the Choctaw's land. About 130 miles farther on was the Choctaw's border with the Chickasaw. Although the Native Americans seldom made serious trouble, they might beg or steal from travelers on the Trace. Some might set travelers' horses free at night, then the next day claim the reward for helping to find the missing animals. The wide and rapidly-flowing Tennessee River marked the boundary between the Chickasaw's land and U. S. territory. Early travelers trying to cross the river had to build makeshift rafts. Later George Colbert, a Chickasaw-Scot, operated a ferry. The cost was fifty cents for a person to cross and one dollar for horse and rider. Legend has it that during the War of 1812 Colbert charged Andrew Jackson $75,000 to provide the general with supplies

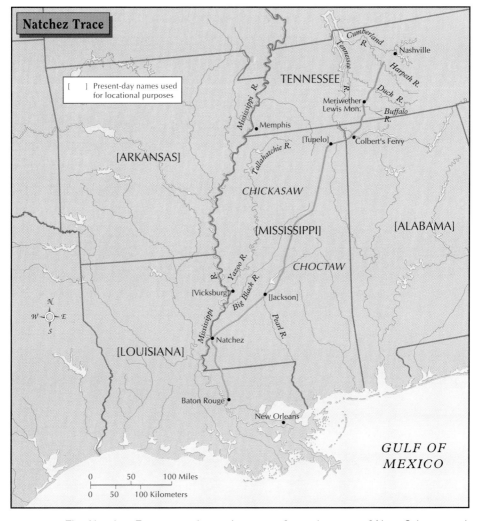

The Natchez Trace was the major route from the area of New Orleans and Baton Rouge north overland to Nashville, Tennessee. The route was used principally by boatmen who had floated boats down the Mississippi and were returning to Ohio and other river ports in the north.

and horses and to ferry his entire army across the river.

The earliest travelers on the Natchez Trace had to camp along the way. Before leaving Natchez they stocked up on provisions for the long journey. Besides dried beef and hard biscuits, they often carried powder of roasted Indian corn. This they made into fritters that were fried in bear oil and sweetened with honey. By the early 1800s a few inns—known as stands—offered plain food and a place to sleep, although often it might be on the floor or on a grassy patch in the garden.

At various times, different European nations controlled the land around Natchez. In 1682 France claimed the area, even though the Spanish had explored it nearly 150 years earlier. When France lost the French and Indian War in 1763, it gave to Great Britain all of its holdings east of the Mississippi River (except New Orleans). At the same time, France gave New Orleans and its holdings west of the Mississippi to Spain.

During the Revolutionary War, Spanish troops occupied the Natchez district and other ports on the lower Mississippi River. After the United States became a nation,

The Louisiana Purchase

In late November of 1803 Spain gave New Orleans and all of the land in the Mississippi Valley west of the Mississippi River to France. Only three weeks later, Napoleon, leader of France, sold this land (known as "Louisiana") to the United States. This was the famous "Louisiana Purchase," which more than doubled the size of the United States and moved the nation's western boundary as far west as the Rocky Mountains.

Spain did not give up this claim. It took another treaty with Spain, in 1795, for people in the United States to be able to float boats down the Mississippi River and deposit their goods in New Orleans.

In 1798, the United States finally took possession of the Natchez district, and regular mail delivery began between Nashville and Natchez. The first postrider, John Swaney, held the job for eight years. He rode about 25 miles in a day,

Europeans on the Trails

The new United States was popular with English tourists. Novelist Charles Dickens was an early visitor. So was the young English astronomer Francis Baily. He followed many of the nation's trails along the east coast by coach and packhorse.

In the winter of 1796 Baily went west by stagecoach to Pittsburgh. There he built a flatboat. He floated down the Ohio River to Cincinnati, then took passage with a flatboat hauling 400 barrels of flour to New Orleans. Since Baily was unable to book passage from New Orleans to New York by ship, he returned to Natchez and from there walked north along the Trace.

He asked five Germans who had also floated south from Pittsburgh to share the lonely walk back up to Nashville. Among provisions they bought for their journey were 15 pounds of biscuit, six pounds of flour, 12 pounds of bacon, ten pounds of dried beef, three pounds of rice, one and a half pounds of coffee, four pounds of sugar, and some pounded (ground) corn with which to make corn cakes (like pancakes).

Through the land of the Chickasaw the Englishman and his companions hired a Native American guide. In Nashville, Baily caught a stagecoach which carried him after considerable time to New York. From there he returned to England on a sailing ship.

and made the round-trip every three weeks. He took along his oil-dressed deerskin mail pouch, a half bushel of corn for his horse, an overcoat, and a tin trumpet to announce his arrival at the end of the line. Most nights he built a fire and slept wrapped in a blanket with a pistol at his side. Often he stayed overnight at George Colbert's stand (inn) on the Tennessee River. When coming south from Nashville, Swaney had to reach the ferry landing before dark. For if he arrived after Colbert's bedtime, the ferryman would refuse to pole his boat over to pick Swaney up.

When a postrider came to a Native American village or white settlement along the trail he always blew the tin trumpet in case someone had mail for him to carry. At the halfway point, the village of the Chickasaw (now Tupelo, Mississippi), the rider changed horses. The ride was long and lonely, and the postrider was grateful for company— except for the time one mail carrier suddenly found himself facing a bandit on the trail. Fortunately the bandit said he was after money, not letters!

In 1801, Congress made plans to improve the Trace. Government officials met with leaders of the Chickasaw and the Choctaw nations since most of the trail ran through their land. At the meeting, both Indian nations agreed to let the Americans build a road if the Native Americans were given the right to operate all of the stands (inns) and all the ferryboats across streams within their lands.

The Chickasaw helped mark the guideline through their territory, and army soldiers set to work on the new road. They improved the ferry landing at Colbert's Ferry on the Tennessee River, but after that progress was slow. With axes and knives the men chopped trees, cut brush, and slashed at the tough grasses along ridges and beside swamps. But soon after vines and bushes were cleared,

This nineteenth century painting shows Choctaws walking along the Natchez Trace.

they grew back thicker than ever. After a year the middle part of the Trace was still a tangle of wilderness where you could hear panthers screaming at night, and gangs of thieves were apt to be lurking in the shadows.

Even though the entire Natchez Trace was never converted into a good road, it was heavily traveled. Despite the hazards of the journey, it was the most popular wilderness road in the Old Southwest. Besides homeward-bound boatmen on the trail were settlers heading south (and a few disappointed ones heading north), preachers, soldiers, bandits, land speculators, and peddlers, their pack animals loaded with linen shirts, calico, mirrors, and similar items for sale.

In 1812 the first steamboat arrived in Natchez. Soon steamboats called regularly at ports up and down the

Lewis on the Natchez Trace

One famous American who lost his life on the "dark and fearsome" Natchez Trace was Meriwether Lewis. Along with William Clark, Lewis had led the Lewis and Clark expedition (1804-1806) to explore the newly-purchased Louisiana Territory west of the Mississippi.

On his return from that journey of discovery, Meriwether Lewis was appointed governor of the new Louisiana Territory. In 1809, he left St. Louis to meet with a congressional committee in Washington. He began his journey by floating down the Mississippi River to Natchez on a flatboat. Then, with his two servants, Lewis started up the Natchez Trace. Packhorses carried his official papers. During a thunderstorm Lewis stopped at Grinder's Inn, a run-down stand on

the Trace about 50 miles south of Nashville. There he died mysteriously, of gunshot wounds. At the time, many people believed he took his own life. Thomas Jefferson also judged it suicide. Since then, it is believed that an assassin probably killed Meriwether Lewis. Today a modern parkway follows the course of the original Natchez Trace. Just west of the parkway at milepost 385.9 along the Old Natchez Trace foot trail a monument marks Lewis's grave.

This plaque and the monument in the background mark the grave of Meriwether Lewis on the Natchez Trace.

In the early nineteenth century steamboats, which could go upstream
as well as downstream, started plying the rivers of the Midwest,
ending the usefulness of the overland Natchez Trace.

Mississippi. With this cheaper, faster way north from
Natchez the heyday of the Natchez Trace was over for
most boatmen. But plenty of others still used the trail,
especially land-hungry easterners looking for a place to
settle. Eventually with the help of the U.S. government
they forced the Chickasaws and the Choctaws to give up
their homeland and move farther west.

In the 1930s government workers began to build a
national road along the old trail. It became the Natchez
Trace Parkway, which extends from the southwest to the
northeast corner of the state of Mississippi and continues
into Tennessee.

EIGHT

The Cumberland/
National Road

The Cumberland Road

In 1784, five years before he became the nation's first President, George Washington met with settlers in what is now West Virginia to talk about the best land route for sending farm produce to markets in the east. Washington knew this area well. Thirty years before, as a young militia officer, he had fought the French here during the French and Indian War. Even earlier he had worked here as a surveyor.

The trail that Washington and the settlers agreed on—which included parts of the old Nemacolin's Path and Braddock's Road—became, 70 years later, the National Road from Cumberland, Maryland to central Illinois.

Thomas Jefferson was President when Congress passed an act in 1803 authorizing the building of a national road. It was to be cleared of trees, raised in the middle with stone, earth, gravel, or sand, and have a ditch for water to run along each side. The national treasury was to pay the chief surveyors four dollars a day, and their helpers between one and three dollars a day.

The first section of the road, known as the Cumberland Road, led from the town of Cumberland on the Potomac River to Wheeling on the Ohio River, 112 miles westward.

In laying out the road the surveyors had to allow room for freight wagons moving in both directions to pass.

Innkeepers, landowners, and factory and mine operators vied to get the road routed through their areas. Surveyors finally chose a route close to existing packhorse trails and river crossings, but with fewer curves and more gradual grades.

Work on the new road began in 1811. Axmen felled trees. Laborers hacked at tree roots. Farmers with teams of oxen hauled earth to fill gullies. Stonemasons shaped stones for culverts and bridges. Within the year the first ten miles were completed. The road was graded and paved

A westward bound wagon passes a tollgate on the Cumberland Road.

with small broken stones packed tightly together. Despite the War of 1812, work on the Cumberland Road continued. It finally reached Wheeling on the Ohio River in 1818.

For a few years, the road went no farther west, but between Cumberland and Wheeling traffic was heavier than ever, with stagecoaches, Conestoga wagons, and pack trains sharing the crowded road with drovers' herds and emigrants' wagons.

At Wheeling, some emigrants heading west loaded their possessions onto flatboats, and drifted down the Ohio River the rest of the way to their new homes. Others stayed with their wagons, crossing the river by ferry and then heading west and then south over the bumpy Zane's Trace toward settlements in southern Ohio or northern Kentucky.

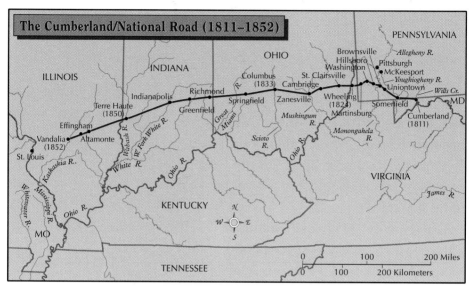

The Cumberland/National Road became a major route west to Illinois
and St. Louis during the first half of the nineteenth century.

The National Road

In 1825 Congress provided funds to extend the road
beyond Wheeling, calling the entire road the National
Road. From Wheeling, it followed the route of Zane's Trace
as far as Zanesville, then continued straight west. It
reached Ohio's capital at Columbus in 1833.

More traffic jammed the road as each new section was
finished. Taverns and inns sprang up beside the road offering accommodations to stagecoach passengers. At night
the freight wagon drivers and drovers camped, or stopped
at special wagon houses that provided wagon yards for the
teams and pasture pens for the drovers' stock. In the main
room of the house a driver could eat a hearty meal for
twelve and a half cents, share songs and stories, or join in
a hoedown (square dance) before unrolling his bedroll to
sleep on the floor next to 20 or 30 other freighters and
drovers.

By 1850 the National Road was completed across Indiana. Two years later it reached Vandalia, the former capital of Illinois. By this time, the eastern sections had been so heavily used that parts of the road had been cut to pieces. Congress refused to pay for the repairs, so the states put up their own tollhouses every few miles, charging fees based on how much damage to expect. The fee for cattle was more than for sheep, since cows' sharp hooves cut deeper holes in the rock paving. Farm wagons with narrow iron wheels that could slash the roadway were charged more than freight wagons with wider wheels. Travel was free if a wagon's wheels were more than eight inches wide, since the wide wheels acted as rollers and did no damage at all to the road.

Fifty years after his death, the trail west that George Washington had suggested was a reality at last. It had taken more than 40 years to build, but the National Road now stretched from the Atlantic coast almost to the Mississippi River.

A contemporary artist's depiction of a wagon train on the National Road.

A Network
of Trails
in the East

O ne year after the Cumberland Road reached Wheeling on the Ohio River, officials in what is now Indiana signed a treaty with the Potawatomis, who agreed to give up a strip of land 100 feet wide from Lake Michigan to the Wabash River, and other sections of good land as well. For this grant the Potawatomis received "goods and privileges" whose value would now be about $114,000.

By reselling the sections of good land to settlers, the people of Indiana made enough money to build a wide road from what is now St. Joseph, in Michigan, through Indianapolis to the Ohio River town of Madison, Indiana. The road was well built, made stronger in many places with seasoned oak timbers laid down and covered with a foot and a half of soil.

The Michigan Road crossed the National Road at Indianapolis, and in the early 1800s it became the main route for settlers traveling between the valley of the Ohio River and Lake Michigan. Combined with the Natchez Trace, the Michigan Road provided an overland trail all the way from New Orleans to the Great Lakes. The eastern half of the United States now had a system of trails and roads that crisscrossed every part of the nation from the Atlantic coast to the western frontier on the Mississippi

The Trail of Tears

By the 1800s, early settlers along the eastern seacoast had already taken over much of what was once Indian territory. As later settlers ventured farther inland they acquired even more Indian land—by treaty, trickery, or even by force.

Finally, in May of 1830, the Congress of the United States passed the Indian Removal Act. This enabled the government to take over all Indian lands east of the Mississippi River by relocating the eastern Indian nations west of the Mississippi. According to terms of the Act, all Native Americans who agreed were to receive some money for their land, travel expenses to Indian Territory (now the state of Oklahoma), and one year's living expenses. Army soldiers would escort them on their journey.

(continued on page 84)

Native Americans from the southeastern United States were accompanied on the "Trail of Tears" by soldiers such as the one in the blue uniform at the left of this painting by Robert Lindveux.

(continued from page 83)

During the next dozen years, bands of Shawnee, Delaware, Wyandot, Seneca, and others were moved west. From a reservation in Alabama came the Creeks. From Mississippi came the Choctaws and the Chickasaws, and from Florida, the Seminoles. Many of the Native Americans had been tricked or coerced into agreeing.

The last to give up their homeland were the Cherokees, whose nation covered parts of Georgia, Alabama, and Tennessee. When the Cherokee families were finally forced to leave, they traveled west by flatboat along rivers, or made the grueling 600-mile overland journey by wagon, on horseback, or on foot. Many suffered greatly on this forced march westward. Thousands died of pneumonia, or from cholera, measles, or other European diseases to which they had no immunity. This tragic journey is now known as "The Trail of Tears."

River, and from the Gulf of Mexico to the border with Canada.

The original plan was to continue building a National Road all the way to St. Louis. But even before the road builders reached the middle of Indiana, many travelers were already choosing a faster and easier way to go west: by train. By 1842, trains of the Baltimore and Ohio Company steamed from Baltimore to Cumberland. A dozen years later, railroad tracks stretched from the east coast all the way to the Mississippi River. The railroad locomotive was rapidly taking over work once done by stagecoach horses and the six-horse teams hitched to Conestoga freight wagons. Except for local traffic, the National Road was nearly deserted.

All of that changed in the late 1800s with the arrival of the gasoline-powered automobile. Again the National Road became crowded, this time with buses, heavy trucks, and passenger cars such as the Model T Ford.

To accommodate the new rush of traffic workmen paved and widened the road and put up road signs. Truck stops, camp sites, and tourist cabins replaced wagon stands and roadside inns.

In 1926 the National Road became part of U.S. Highway 40. Today you can still follow U.S. 40 west from Baltimore to St. Louis (and beyond). Along the way you will see a few tollgate houses and old inns as well as historical landmarks such as the reconstructed Fort Necessity, built by Lt. George Washington at the beginning of the French and Indian War.

Glossary

Appalachians Chain of eastern mountains that extend from Quebec to Alabama.

bateau Light, flat-bottomed boat with pointed bow (front) and stern (back); French word meaning "boat."

blaze Chip a mark on a tree.

Boone's Trace First name for Wilderness Road.

Conestoga wagon Brightly-painted freight wagons of the 1700s, with curved body, canvas covers, and wide, heavy wheels and drawn by teams of five or six horses or oxen.

corduroy road Rough road, usually over muddy areas, made by placing logs close together.

drover Herder of cattle, sheep, or other animals.

dugout canoe Canoe made by hollowing out a log.

emigrant One who leaves home to live elsewhere, such as early settlers who came to North America from Europe, and those settlers in the east who moved westward.

flatboat Large boat with flat bottom, used on rivers to haul freight.

flax Plant whose fibers are used to make thread for weaving cloth.

flying column Especially fast-moving foot soldiers.

forge Open fireplace for heating metal.

fur trade Business of exchanging pelts of beaver and other animals for money or goods.

king's highway Main roads in American colonies during time colonists were still ruled by England's king.

land grants Tracts of land once belonging to Indian tribes that were given to individuals by the United States government.

long hunter Woodsmen (such as Daniel Boone) who left their home and family for months, or even years, to wander beyond the frontier in search of game and adventure.

"longhouse" Native American term for land in what is now New York State where Five Nations Confederacy (the Iroquois) lived in peace and harmony in the 1500s.

macadam Stone broken into small pieces (later combined with cement or asphalt) to form a solid hard road surface.

milestone Stone placed to mark distance in miles from a town; Benjamin Franklin started use of milestones in 1751 to establish postage for letters.

molten Made liquid by heat (such as molten iron).

musket Gun with long, smooth barrel, used from 1500s to late 1700s.

Northwest Ordinance 1787 U.S. Government ordinance that allowed settlers in Northwest Territory (later known as "Old Northwest" and also "Ohio Country"; territory included what are now states of Ohio, Michigan, Indiana, Illinois, Wisconsin and part of Minnesota); the ordinance also promised that Indian lands and property would never be taken from them without their permission.

Ohio Valley Valley of the Ohio River, which flows from western Pennsylvania to the Mississippi River.

"Pennsylvania Dutch" Language that was a mixture of German and English, spoken by German emigrants in and around Lancaster County, Pennsylvania.

"pigs" or pig iron Crude iron bars made from molten iron.

portage Land trail between waterways.

Quaker Member of the Society of Friends, a religious sect opposed to war.

Quebec A fortified town on the St. Lawrence River in Canada, occupied by the French until the British claimed it in 1759.

salt lick Place near salt springs where earth and rocks become encrusted with salt.

"shunpike" Pathway leading around a tollhouse, used by those who wanted to avoid paying toll.

slaughterhouse A place where animals are butchered.

stands Name for inns on Natchez Trace.

stores Supplies of food, clothing, guns, and ammunition.

surveyor One who determines boundaries, area, and elevations of land by measuring angles and distances.

swivel gun Gun that rotates by turning on a pivot.

tavern Along early eastern roads, an inn for travelers

teamster Wagon driver.

totem An animal, plant, or natural object—or its mark—that serves as emblem of a clan, family, or tribe.

trace Path or trail formed by passage of animals or people.

Warrior's Path (or Great Warrior's Path) North-south trail through Appalachians used by the Cherokee and other Indians between homes and hunting grounds in what are now Kentucky and Tennessee.

Further Reading

Altsheler, Joseph A. *Kentucky Frontiersmen: The Adventures of Henry Ware, Hunter and Border Fighter.* Voyageur Pub., 1988

American Way West. Facts on File, 1990

Anderson, Joan W. *Pioneer Children of Appalachia.* Houghton Mifflin, 1990

Bradfield, Carl. *Tecumseh's Trail: The Appalachian Trail, Then and Now.* ASDA Pub.

Callaway, Colin G. *Indians of the Northeast.* Facts on File, 1991

Cavan, Seamus. *Daniel Boone and the Opening of the Ohio Country.* Chelsea House, 1991

Crump, Donald, J., ed. *Pathways to Discovery: Exploring America's National Trails.* National Geographic Society, 1990

Egloff, Keith & Woodward, Deborah, eds. *First People: The Early Indians of Virginia.* University Press of Virginia, 1992

Harper, Jon. *Blue Ridge.* Our Child Press, 1995

Holler, Anne. *Chief Powhatan and Pocahontas.* Chelsea House, 1993

Lawlor, Laurie. *Daniel Boone.* Whitman, Albert & Co., 1989

Mancini, Richard E. *Indians of the Southeast.* Facts on File, 1991

McCall, Edith. *Biography of a River: The Mississippi.* Walker & Co., 1990

McNeese, Tim. *America's Early Canals.* Macmillan, 1993

———— *Conestogas and Stagecoaches.* Macmillan, 1993

———— *From Trails to Turnpikes.* Macmillan, 1993

Meyers, Madeleine, intro. *Cherokee Nation; Life Before the Tears.* Discovery Enterprises, Ltd., 1993

Oxlade, Chris. *Canals and Waterways.* Franklin Watts, 1994

Siegel, Beatrice. *Fur Trappers and Traders: The Indians, the Pilgrims, and the Beavers.* Walker & Co., 1987

Spangenburg, Ray and Moser, Diane. *The Story of America's Roads.* Facts on File, 1991

Twist, Clint. *Lewis and Clark: Exploring North America.* Raintree Steck-Vaughn, 1994

Weinberg, Karen. *Cherokee Passage.* White Mane, 1995

Bibliography

* Indicates book of special interest to young adult readers

*Armento, Beverly J., Nash, Gary B., Salter, Christopher L., Wixson, Karen K., *A More Perfect Union*, Boston: Houghton Mifflin Co., 1994.

Bailey, Kenneth P., *The Ohio Company of Virginia and the Westward Movement 1748-1792*, Glendale, Calif.: The Arthur H. Clark Co., 1939.

Bruce, H. Addington, *Daniel Boone & The Wilderness Road*, New York: The MacMillan Co., 1910.

Carter, Hodding, *Lower Mississippi (Rivers of America Series)*, New York: Farrar & Rinehart, Inc., 1942.

Caruso, John A., *The Appalachian Frontier: America's First Surge Westward*, Indianapolis: The Bobbs-Merrill Co., Inc., 1959.

Coates, Robert M., *The Outlaw Years*, New York: The Literary Guild of America, 1930.

Cochran, Thomas C. *Pennsylvania*, New York: W. W. Norton & Co., 1978.

Coleman, R. V., *The First Frontier*, New York: Charles Scribner's Sons, 1948.

Connecticut: A Guide to its Roads, Lore, and People (WPA Writer's Project), Boston: Houghton Mifflin Company, 1938.

*Daniels, Jonathan, *The Devil's Backbone, the Story of the Natchez Trace (American Trail Series)*, New York: McGraw-Hill Book Co., 1962.

*Faragher, John Mack, *Daniel Boone*, New York: Henry Holt & Co., 1992.

Faris, John T., *Old Roads Out of Philadelphia*, Philadelphia: J.B. Lippincott Co., 1917.

Georgia (American Guide Series), Athens: Univ. of Georgia Press, 1940.

Harrington, M. R., *The Iroquois Trail*, New Brunswick: Rutgers Univer. Press, 1991.

Historical Statistics of the United States: Colonial Times to 1970, PART 1, Washington D.C.: US Dept. of Commerce, Bureau of the Census, 1975

*Holbrook, Stewart H., *The Old Post Road: The Story of the Boston Post Road (American Trail Series)*, New York: McGraw-Hill Book Co., Inc., 1962.

Hulbert, Archer Butler, *Historic Highways of America, vol.2, Indian Thoroughfares*, Cleveland Ohio: The Arthur H. Clark Company, 1904.

—————— *The Paths of Inland Commerce*, New Haven: Yale Univ. Press, 1920

Keir, Malcolm, *The March of Commerce*, New Haven: Yale Univ. Press., 1927.

Kincaid, Robert L., *The Wilderness Road (The American Trails Series)*, Indianapolis: Bobbs-Merrill Co., 1947.

Maine: A Guide 'Down East', Rockland, Maine: Courier-Gazette, Inc., 1970.

Massachusetts (The WPA Guide to...), New York: Pantheon Books, 1983.

Morison, Samuel Eliot, *The Oxford History of the American People*, New York: Oxford University Press, 1965.

New York (American Guide Series), New York: The Oxford Univ.Press, 1940.

Ohio Guide (American Guide Series), New York: Oxford Univ.Press, 1943.

Schneider, Norris F., *The National Road: Main Street of America*, Columbus, Ohio: Ohio Historical Society, 1975.

*Wright, Richardson, *Hawkers & Walkers in Early America*, Philadelphia: J.B. Lippincott Company, 1927.

Index

Note: Page numbers in italics indicate maps; numbers in bold indicate illustrations.